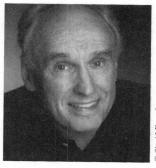

© Sigrid Estrada

FRANK BIDART

Watching the Spring Festival

Frank Bidart's most recent full-length collections of poetry are *Star Dust* (FSG, 2005), *Desire* (FSG, 1997), and *In the Western Night: Collected Poems 1965–90* (FSG, 1990). He has won many prizes, including, most recently, the 2007 Bollingen Prize for Poetry. He teaches at Wellesley College.

WATCHING THE SPRING FESTIVAL

WATCHING THE SPRING FESTIVAL

Frank Bidart

Farrar, Straus and Giroux
New York

Farrar, Straus and Giroux
18 West 18th Street, New York 10011

Copyright © 2008 by Frank Bidart
All rights reserved
Distributed in Canada by Douglas & McIntyre Ltd.
Printed in the United States of America
Published in 2008 by Farrar, Straus and Giroux
First paperback edition, 2009

Grateful acknowledgment is made to the following publications, in which
some of these poems first appeared: The American Scholar, Arrowsmith
Press ("Coat," broadside), Boston Review, High Chair, The New Yorker
("An American in Hollywood," "Marilyn Monroe," "To the Republic"),
Ploughshares, Poetry ("If See No End In Is," "The Old Man at the
Wheel," "Ulanova At Forty-Six At Last Dances Before a Camera
Giselle"), Salmagundi, The Threepenny Review.

The Library of Congress has cataloged the hardcover edition as follows:
Bidart, Frank, 1939–
    Watching the spring festival / Frank Bidart. — 1st ed.
       p.   cm.
    ISBN-13: 978-0-374-28603-3 (alk. paper)
    ISBN-10: 0-374-28603-5 (alk. paper)
    I. Title.

    PS3552.I33W38 2008
    811'.54—dc22

                                                    2007040513

Paperback ISBN-13: 978-0-374-53172-0
Paperback ISBN-10: 0-374-53172-2

www.fsgbooks.com

10   9   8   7   6   5   4   3   2   1

CONTENTS

WATCHING THE
SPRING FESTIVAL

MARILYN MONROE

Because the pact beneath ordinary life (*If you
give me enough money, you can continue to fuck me—*)

induces in each person you have ever known
panic and envy before the abyss,

what you come from is craziness, what your
mother and her mother come from is

craziness, panic of the animal
smelling what you have in store for it.

Your father's name, she said, is too
famous not to be hidden.

Kicking against the pricks,
she somehow injured her mind.

You are bitter all that releases
transformation in us is illusion.

Poor, you thought being rich is utterly
corrosive; and watched with envy.

Posing in the garden,
squinting into the sun.

TU FU WATCHES THE SPRING FESTIVAL ACROSS SERPENTINE LAKE

In 753 Tu Fu, along with a crowd of others, watched the imperial court—the emperor's mistress, her sisters, the first minister—publicly celebrate the advent of spring.

Intricate to celebrate still-delicate
raw spring, peacocks in *passement* of gold

thread, unicorns embroidered palely in silver.
These are not women but a dream of women:—

bandeaux of kingfisher-feather

                    jewelry, pearl

netting that clings to the breathing body

veil what is, because touched earth
is soiled earth, invisible.

As if submission to dream were submission
not only to breeding but to one's own nature,

what is gorgeous is remote now, pure, true.

                    •

The Mistress of the Cloud-Pepper Apartments
has brought life back to the emperor, who is

old. Therefore charges of gross extravagance, of
pandering incest between her sister Kuo and her cousin

are, in the emperor's grateful eyes, unjust. Her wish
made her cousin first minister. Three springs from this

spring, the arrogance of the new first minister
will arouse such hatred and fury even the frightened

emperor must accede to his execution. As bitterly to
hers. She will be carried on a palanquin of

plain wood to a Buddhist chapel
deep in a wood and strangled.

                  .

Now the Mistress of the Cloud-Pepper Apartments, —
whose rooms at her insistence are coated with

a pepper-flower paste into which dried pepper-
flowers are pounded because the rooms of the Empress

always are coated with paste into which dried pepper-
flowers are pounded and she is Empress

now in all but name, — is encircled by her
sisters, Duchesses dignified by imperial

favor with the names of states that once had
power, Kuo, Ch'in, Han. Now rhinoceros-horn

chopsticks, bored, long have not descended.
The belled carving knife wastes its labors. Arching

camel humps, still perfect, rise like purple hills
from green-glazed cauldrons. Wave after

wave of imperial eunuchs, balancing fresh
delicacies from the imperial kitchens, gallop up

without stirring dust.

                    •

With mournful sound that would move demon
gods, flutes and drums now declare to the air

he is arrived. Dawdlingly

                    he arrives, as if the cloud of

suppliants clinging to him cannot obscure the sun.

Power greater than that of all men except one
knows nothing worth rushing toward

or rushing from. Finally the new first minister
ascends the pavilion. He greets the Duchess of

Kuo with that slight
brutality intimacy induces.

Here at last is power that your
soul can warm its hands against!

Beware: success has made him
incurious, not less dangerous.

(AFTER TU FU,
"Ballad of Lovely Women")

THE OLD MAN AT THE WHEEL

Measured against the immeasurable
universe, no word you have spoken

brought light. Brought
light to what, as a child, you thought

too dark to be survived. *By exorcism
you survived. By submission, then making.*

You let all the parts of that thing you would
cut out of you enter your poem because

enacting there all its parts allowed you
the illusion you could cut it from your soul.

Dilemmas of choice given what cannot
change alone roused you to words.

As you grip the things that were young when
you were young, they crumble in your hand.

Now you must drive west, which in November
means driving directly into the sun.

This age that has tried to use indeterminacy
to imagine we are free

Days and nights typing and retyping

revisions half in
relish because what you have

made is ill-made

•

Picking up the phone next to your bed
when her voice said he is dead you

stood up on your bed

Like lightning across an open field
I he said

wound the ground

•

His body had risen up to kill him
because beneath him there was no

earth where the soul could stand

9

·

Renewed health and renewed illness
meant the freedom

or necessity to risk a new life

Bar by bar he built meticulously
a new cage to escape each cage he built

why why why why

It is an illusion you were ever free

The voice of the bird you could not help
but respond to

The trick was to give yourself only to what
could not receive what you had to give,

leaving you as you wished, free.
Still you court the world by enacting yet once

more the ecstatic rituals of enthrallment.
You cannot rest. The great grounding

events in your life (weight lodged past
change, like the sweetest, most fantastical myth

enshrining yet enslaving promise), the great
grounding events that left you so changed

you cannot conceive your face without their
happening, happened when someone

could receive. Just as she once did, he did—past
judgment of pain or cost. Could receive. Did.

POEM ENDING WITH THREE LINES FROM "HOME ON THE RANGE"

Barred from the pool twenty-three years ago, still I dove
straight in. You loved to swim, but saw no water.

Whenever Ray Charles sings "I Can't Stop Loving You"

I can't stop loving you. Whenever the unstained-by-guilt
cheerful chorus belts out the title, as his voice, sweet

and haggard reminder of what can never be remedied,

answers, correcting the children with "It's useless to say,"
the irreparable enters me again, again me it twists.

The red man was pressed from this part of the West—

'tis unlikely he'll ever return to the banks of Red River, where
seldom, if ever, their flickering campfires burn.

After you were bitten by a wolf and transformed
into a monster who feeds on other human beings

each full moon and who, therefore, in disgust

wants to die, you think *The desire to die is not
feeling suicidal. It abjures mere action. You have*

wanted to die since the moment you were born.

Crazy narratives—that lend what is merely
in you, and therefore soon-to-be-repeated,

the fleeting illusion of logic and cause.

You think *Those alive there, in the glowing rectangle,
lead our true lives! They have not, as we have been*

forced to here, cut off their arms and legs.

There, you dance as well as Fred Astaire,
though here, inexplicably, you cannot.

Sewer. Still black water

above whose mirror
you bend your face. Font.

SEDUCTION

Show him that you see he carries
always, everywhere, an enormous

almost impossible to balance or bear

statue of himself: burden that
flattering him

dwarfs him, like you. Make him

see that you alone decipher within him
the lineaments of the giant. Make him

see that you alone can help him shape

the inchoate works of his hand, till what
the statue is he is. *He watches your helpless*

gaze; your gaze

tells him that the world someday must see.
You are the dye whose color dyes

the mirror: he can never get free.

•

You ask what is this place. He says
kids come to make out here. He has driven

out here to show you lovers' lane.

Because your power in the world exceeds
his, he must make the first move.

His hand on the car seat doesn't move.

•

He is Ralegh attending Elizabeth, still
able to disguise that he does not want her.

In banter and sweet colloquy, he freely,

abundantly shows you that what his
desire is is endless

intercourse with your soul. Everything

he offers, by intricate
omissions, displays what he denies you.

Beneath all, the *no* that you

persuade yourself
can be reversed.

•

You cannot reverse it: as if he is

safe from
engulfment only because he has

placed past reversal

the judgment that each
animal makes facing another.

You are an animal facing another.

               •

Still you persuade yourself that it can be
reversed because he teasingly sprinkles

evasive accounts of his erotic history

with tales of dissatisfying but repeated
sex with men. He adds that he

could never fall in love with a man.

Helplessly, he points to the soiled
statue he strains to hold

unstained above him. He cannot.

               •

You must write this without the least
trace of complaint. Standing at the edge of

the pool, for him there was no water.

You chose him not despite, but
because of. In the twenty-three years since

breaking with him, his spectre

insists that no one ever replaces anyone.
He is the dye whose color dyes

the mirror: you can never get free.

•

What is it that impels

What is it that impels us at least in
imagination

What is it that impels us at least in

imagination to close with to
interpenetrate flesh that accepts

craves interpenetration from

us with us
What is it What

•

Sweet cow, to heal the world, you must

jump over the moon. All you ask is
immolation, fantastic love resistlessly

drawn out of a withdrawn creature who

must turn himself inside out to give it:
dream coexistent with breathing.

•

Near the end, when the old absorbing

colloquy begins again, both he and you
find yourselves surrounded by ash.

To his meagre circumscribed desire whose

no you knew from the beginning, that you
want to pluck out of your eye forever,

you submit as if in mourning.

To ash, he too submits. In revenge
you chose submission, chose power.

What I hate I love. Ask the crucified hand that holds
the nail that now is driven into itself, why.

The desire to approach obliteration
preexists each metaphysic justifying it. Watch him
fucked want to get fucked hard. Christianity

allowed the flagellants

light, for even Jesus found release from flesh requires
mortification of the flesh. From the ends of
the earth the song is, *Grind me into dust.*

VALENTINE

How those now dead used the word *love* bewildered
and disgusted the boy who resolved he

would not reassure the world he felt
love until he understood love

Resolve that too soon crumbled when he found
within his chest

something intolerable for which the word
because no other word was right

must be love
must be love

Love craved and despised and necessary
the Great American Songbook said explained our fate

my bereft grandmother bereft
father bereft mother their wild regret

How those now dead used love to explain
wild regret

WITH EACH FRESH DEATH THE SOUL
REDISCOVERS WOE

from the world that called you Piñon not one voice is now not stopped
Piñon little pine nut sweet seed of the pine tree which is evergreen

Soul that discovered itself as it discovered the irreparable

breaking through ice to touch the rushing stream whose skin
breaking allowed darkness to swallow blondhaired Ramona

in 1944 age six high in the cold evergreen Sierras as you

age five luckily were elsewhere but forever after Soul there
failing to pull her for years of nights from the irreparable

SANJAYA AT 17

As if fearless what the shutter will unmask
he offers himself to the camera, to
us, sheerly—
vulnerable like Monroe, like Garbo.

Now he is a cock that raises
high above his wagging head
the narrow erected red
flag of arousal—

Of course the ignorant, you say, *hate him.*
In the world's long conversation, long
warfare about essence, each taunting
song, each disarming photograph, a word.

There is a creature, among all others, one,
within whose voice there is a secret voice
which once heard
unlocks the door that unlocks the mountain.

Like the invisible seasons

Which dye then bury all the eye
sees, but themselves cannot be seen

Out of ceaseless motion in edgeless space

Inside whatever muck makes words in
lines leap into being is the intimation of

Like the invisible seasons

Process, inside chaos you follow the thread
of just one phrase instinct with cycle, archaic

Out of ceaseless motion in edgeless space

Promise that you will see at last the buried
snake that swallows its own tail

Like the invisible seasons

You believe not in words but in words in
lines, which disdaining the right margin

Out of ceaseless motion in edgeless space

Inside time make the snake made out of
time pulse without cease electric in space

Like the invisible seasons

Though the body is its
genesis, a poem is the vision of a process

Out of ceaseless motion in edgeless space

Carved in space, vision your poor eye's single
armor against winter spring summer fall

ULANOVA AT FORTY-SIX AT LAST DANCES
BEFORE A CAMERA GISELLE

Many ways to dance Giselle, but tonight as you
watch you think that she is what art is, creature

who remembers

her every gesture and senses its relation to the time
just a moment before when she did something

close to it

but then everything was different so what she feels
now is the pathos of the difference. Her body

hopping forward

remembers the pathos of the difference. Each
hop is small, but before each landing she has

stepped through

many ghosts. This and every second is the echo
of a second like it but different when you had

illusions not

only about others but about yourself. Each gesture
cuts through these other earlier moments to exist as

a new gesture

but carries with it all the others, so what you dance
is the circle or bubble you carry that is all this.

•

Inside the many ways to dance Giselle

the single way that will show those who sleep what
tragedy is. What tragedy is is

your work in Act One. Then comes something else.

•

The poem I've never been able to write has a very tentative title:
"Ulanova At Forty-Six At Last Dances Before a Camera Giselle."
A nice story about an innocent who dies because tricked by the
worldly becomes, with Ulanova, tragedy. A poem about being in
normal terms too old to dance something but the world wants to
record it because the world knows that it is precious but you also
know the camera is good at unmasking those who are too old to
create the illusion on which every art in part depends. About
burning an image into the soul of an eighteen-year-old (me) of the
severity and ferocity at the root of classic art, addicted to mimesis.

•

After her entrance, applause. We are watching

a stage production, filmed one act per
night after an earlier public performance.

But without an audience, who is applauding?

The clapping is
artifice, added later. We are watching

the illusion of a stage performance, filmed

by Mr. Paul Czinner using techniques he specially
developed to record the Bolshoi Ballet's first

appearance in the west. Despite the Iron

Curtain, at the height of the Cold War, the Russian
government now has decreed we may see Ulanova.

                    •

Whether out of disgust or boredom, the young

Duke of Silesia has buried what the world
understands as his identity

here, in a rural dream. Watching her

from the safety of his disguise
he is charmed: he smiles. She is a bird whose

wings beat so swiftly they are invisible.

•

Tragedy begins with a *radical given*—your uncle has murdered your father and married your mother. Before your birth a prophecy that you will kill your father and marry your mother leads your father to decree your murder. The *radical given*— irremediable, inescapable—lays bare the war that is our birth-right. *Giselle* begins with the premise of an operetta: a duke is in love with a peasant girl.

•

Impossible not to reach for, to touch
what you find is beautiful,

but had not known before existed.

•

. . . The princess. *Her brocaded dress, cloth of*
gold. Behind her back and

embarrassingly before everyone, Giselle

cannot resist caressing it. *Her dangling,*
glittering necklace. Out of graciousness or

condescension, the princess

removed it from her neck, then so
everyone could see, placed it

around yours. How pleased you were!

·

. . . Or Albrecht, stranger, clear
spirit, to whom despite your

dread you gave your heart.

·

Impossible — ; *to your shame.*

·

The princess, to whom Albrecht is betrothed, arrives in the village
during a hunt and takes rest in Giselle's home. A young forester,
jealously in love with Giselle, now finds Albrecht's hidden silver
sword and betrays his secret. Albrecht tries to hide his real status,
but the returning princess greets him affectionately, thus proving
his true identity. Heartbroken by his duplicity, Giselle goes mad
and dies.

·

The Nineteenth Century did not discover but

made ripe the Mad Scene, gorgeous
delirium rehearsing at luxuriant but

momentary length the steps, the undeflectable

stages by which each brilliant light
finds itself extinguished. *She stares*

straight ahead at what her empty hands

still number, still fondle.
Such burning is eager to be extinguished.

.

Before her she can see the hand

that reaches into her
cage

closing over her. *The hand is the future*

devoid of what, to her
horror, she had reached for.

As the future closes over her

the creature inside beating its wings in
panic is dead.

.

You have spent your life writing tragedies for a world that does not
believe in tragedy. What is tragedy? Everyone is born somewhere:
into this body, this family, this place. Into the mystery of your own
predilections that change as you become conscious of what gov-

erns choice, but change little. Into, in short, particularity insepara-
ble from existence. Each particularity, inseparable from its history,
offers and denies. There is a war between each offer you embrace
and what each embrace precludes, what its acceptance denies
you. Most of us blunt and mute this war in order to survive. In
tragedy the war is lived out. The *radical given* cannot be evaded or
erased. No act of intelligence or prowess or cunning or goodwill
can reconcile the patrimony of the earth.

•

Act Two, because this *Giselle* has been
abbreviated by L. Lavrovsky, is a sketch of Act Two.

Worse than being dead yourself

is to imagine him dead.
Many ways to dance Giselle, but in the queer

moonlit halflife of the forest

at night, when Giselle in death
dances with Albrecht to save him, Ulanova

executes the classic postures of ecstasy, of

yearning for
union, as if impersonally—

as if the event were not at last

again to touch him, but pre-ordained,
beyond the will, fixed as the stars are fixed.

.

Here, in darkness, in the queer halflife of

remorse, Myrtha, Queen of the *Wilis*, offers
revenge against those who condemned

you forever to remain unchosen, baffled.

Myrtha, refugee from Ovid famished
into sovereign self-parody by

centuries of refusal and hunger, rules

row upon symmetrical row of pitiless
well-schooled virgins, dressed in white.

Their rigid geometry mocks

ballet as the abode of Romantic
purity, harmonious dream.

.

The conscience-stricken duke visits Giselle's grave and is con-
fronted by the *Wilis*. The Queen condemns him to dance until he
dies. The ghost of Giselle appears and pleads for his life—without
success. Giselle, determined to save him, dances in his place

whenever he falters, allowing him time to recover. The church bell rings: dawn. The power of the *Wilis* is broken.

•

When Giselle dead defies her dead sisters

Death and the dramatist make visible
the pitiless logic within love's *must.*

Love must silence its victims, —
. . . or become their vessel.

She has become his vessel.

•

At dawn, in triumph incapable of youth's
adamant poise, Giselle reenters the ground.

•

"You see how keen the pointed foot looks in the air, during attitudes, arabesques, and passés, how clearly the leg defines and differentiates the different classic shapes. Below the waist Ulanova is a strict classicist; above the waist she alters the shape of classic motions now slightly, now quite a lot, to specify a nuance of drama. Neither element—the lightness below or the weight above—is weakened for the sake of the other." (Edwin Denby)

•

Ulanova came to Pomona California in

1957 as light projected on a screen

to make me early in college see what art is.

[   ] or full feeling return to my legs.

My jealous, arrogant, offended by existence
soul, as the body allowing you breath

erodes under you, you are changed —

the fewer the gestures that can, in the future,
be, the sweeter those left to you to make.

CANDIDATE

on each desk mantel refrigerator door

an array of photographs
little temple of affections

you have ironically but patiently made

.

Those promises that make us confront
our ambition, pathetic ambition:

confront it best when we see what it
promised die. Your dead ex-wife

you put back on the mantel
when your next wife left. With her iron

nasals, Piaf regrets NOTHING: crazed
by the past, the sweet desire to return to

zero. Undisenthralled you
regret what could not have been

otherwise and remain itself.
There, the hotel in whose bar you courted

both your wives is detonated, collapsing;
in its ballroom, you conceded the election.

There's your open mouth
conceding.

A good photograph tells you everything
that's really going on is invisible.

You are embarrassed by so many
dead flowers. They lie shriveled before you.

COAT

You, who never lied, lied
about what you at every moment carried.

The shameful, new, incomprehensible

disease which you whose religion was
candor couldn't bear not to hide.

Now that you have been dead thirteen years

I again see you suddenly lay out my coat
across your bed, caressing it as if touch could

memorize it — no, you're flattening, then

smoothing its edges until under your
hand as I watch it becomes

hieratic, an icon.

What I seized on as promise
was valediction.

I dreamt I saw a caravan of the dead
start out again from Gettysburg.

Close-packed upright in rows on railcar flat-
beds in the sun, they soon will stink.

Victor and vanquished shoved together, dirt
had bleached the blue and gray one color.

Risen again from Gettysburg, as if
the state were shelter crawled to through

blood, risen disconsolate that we
now ruin the great work of time,

they roll in outrage across America.

You betray us is blazoned across each chest.
To each eye as they pass: *You betray us.*

Assaulted by the impotent dead, I say it's
their misfortune and none of my own.

I dreamt I saw a caravan of the dead
move on wheels touching rails without sound.

To each eye as they pass: *You betray us.*

(2005)

GOD'S CATASTROPHE IN OUR TIME

when those who decree decree the immemorial

mere habits of the tribe
law established since the foundations of the world

when the brutalities released by
belief engender in you disgust for God

hear the answering baritone sweetness of Mahler's "Urlicht"

I am from God and shall return
to God for this disfiguring

flesh is not light and
from light I am light

when I had eyes what did I do with sight

To see the topography of a dilemma

through the illusion of
hearing, hearing the voices

of those who, like you, must live there.

        •

We are not belated: we stand in an original
relation to the problems of making

art, just as each artist before us did.

At the threshold
you can see the threshold: —

it is a precipice.

When I was young, I tried not to
generalize; I had seen little. At sixty-six,

you have done whatever you do

many times before. Disgust with mimesis, —
disgust with the banality of naturalistic

representation, words mere surface mirroring

a surface, —
is as necessary as mimesis: as the conventions

the world offers out of which to construct your

mirror fail, to see your face you
intricately, invisibly reinvent them. But

imagining that words must make the visible

a little hard to see, —
or speech that imitates for the ear speech

now is used up, the ground sealed off from us, —

is a sentimentality. Stevens was wrong. Genius
leading the disgusted over a cliff.

Everything made is made out of its

refusals: those who follow make it new
by refusing its refusals.

The French thought Shakespeare

a barbarian, because in their eyes he wrote as if
ignorant of decorum, remaking art to cut through.

WATCHING THE SPRING FESTIVAL

In my dreams all I need to do is bend
my head, and you well up beneath me

We have been present at a great abundance

displayed beneath glass, sealed beneath
glass as if to make earth envy earth

Until my mouth touched the artful

cunning of glass
I was not poor

We have been present at a great abundance

electric on shimmering glass, floating
world that parades before us

saying this is how to parade

Warring priests of transformation, each
animated by an ecstatic secret, insist

they will teach me how to smash the glass

We have been present at a great abundance
which is the source of fury

HYMN

Earth, O fecund, thou. Evanescent when grasped, when

Venus drives all creatures crazy with desire
to couple and in coupling fill the earth with presences

like themselves
needful, ghostly.

                    Earth, O fecund, thou. Electric ghosts

people the horizon, beguiling since childhood
this son of the desert about to disappear.

They are no less loved and feared because
evanescent. Earth, O fecund, thou.

What none knows is when, not if.
Now that your life nears its end
when you turn back what you see
is ruin. You think, It is a prison. No,
it is a vast resonating chamber in
which each thing you say or do is

new, but the same. *What none knows is*
how to change. Each plateau you reach, if
single, limited, only itself, in-
cludes traces of all the others, so that in the end
limitation frees you, there is no
end, if you once see what is there to see.

You cannot see what is there to see —
not when she whose love you failed is
standing next to you. Then, as if refusing the know-
ledge that life unseparated from her is death, as if
again scorning your refusals, she turns away. The end
achieved by the unappeased is burial within.

Familiar spirit, within whose care I grew, within
whose disappointment I twist, may we at last see
by what necessity the double-bind is in the end
the figure for human life, why what we love is
precluded always by something else we love, as if
each no we speak is yes, each yes no.

The prospect is mixed but elsewhere the forecast is no
better. The eyrie where you perch in
exhaustion has food and is out of the wind, if
cold. You feel old, young, old, young: you scan the sea
for movement, though the promise of sex or food is
the prospect that bewildered you to this end.

Something in you believes that it is not the end.
When you wake, sixth grade will start. The finite you know
you fear is infinite: even at eleven, what you love is
what you should not love, which endless bullies in-
tuit unerringly. The future will be different: you cannot see
the end. What none knows is when, not if.

SONG

At night inside in the light

when history
is systole
diastole

awake I am the moment between.

At night when I fold my limbs up
till they fit
in the tiniest box

I am a multiple of zero.

In the sun
even a tick
feeding on blood

to his sorrow becomes visible.

A bat who grows in love with the sun
becomes sick unless disabused of the illusion
he and the sun are free.

Surreal God

you too a multiple of zero
you who make
all roads lead nowhere

Surreal God

I find nothing
except you
beautiful.

When thus in ecstasy I lie to the god of

necessity he replies the world he has devised is
a labyrinth where travelers at last achieve to their
dismay eternal safety in eternal night.

Columbus is dead

so try as you will
you cannot make me feel
embarrassment

at what I find beautiful.

COLLECTOR

As if these vessels by which the voices of
the dead are alive again

were something on which to dream, without

which you cannot dream—
without which you cannot, hoarder, breathe.

Tell yourself what you hoard

commerce or rectitude cannot withdraw.
Your new poem must, you suspect, steal from

The Duchess of Malfi. Tonight, alone, reread it.

.

By what steps can the Slave become
the Master, and is

becoming the master its only release?

It is not release. When your stepfather
went broke, you watched as your mother's

money allowed survival—

It is not release. You watched her pay him
back by multitudinous

daily humiliations. In the back seat of

the car you were terrified as Medea
invented new ways to tell

Jason what he had done to her.

•

You cannot tell that it is there
but it is there, falling.

Once you leave any surface

uncovered for a few hours
you see you are blind.

Your arm is too heavy to wipe

away what falls on a lifetime's
accumulations. The rituals

you love imply that, repeating them,

you store seeds that promise
the end of ritual. Not this. Wipe this

away, tomorrow it is back.

•

The curator, who thinks he made his soul
choosing each object that he found he chose,

wants to burn down the museum.

•

Stacked waist-high along each
increasingly unpassable

corridor, whole lifeworks

wait, abandoned or mysteriously
never even tested by your

promiscuous, ruthless attention.

•

The stratagems by which briefly you
ameliorated, even seemingly

untwisted what still twists within you—

you loved their taste and lay there
on your side

nursing like a puppy.

•

Lee Wiley, singing in your bathroom
about "ghosts in a lonely parade,"

is herself now one—

erased era you loved, whose maturity
was your youth, whose blindnesses

you became you by loathing.

•

Cities at the edge of the largest
holes in the ground

are coastal: the rest, inland.

The old age you fear is Lady
Macbeth wiping away

what your eyes alone can see.

Each of us knows that there is a black
hole within us. No place you hole up is

adequately inland.

•

The song that the dead sing is at one
moment as vivid, various, multi-voiced

as the dead were living —

then violated the next moment, flattened
by the need now to speak in

such a small space, you.

•

He no longer arrives even
in dreams.

You learned love is addiction

when he to whom you spoke on
the phone every day

dying withdrew his voice —

more than friends, but
less than lovers.

There, arranged in a pile, are his letters.

•

The law is that you
must live

in the house you have built.

The law is absurd: it is
written down nowhere.

You are uncertain what crime

is, though each life writhing to
elude what it has made

feels like punishment.

·

Tell yourself, again, *The rituals
you love imply that, repeating them,*

you store seeds that promise

the end of ritual. You store
seeds. Tell yourself, again,

what you store are seeds.

NOTES

"Marilyn Monroe": Throughout, "she" is Monroe's mother. She was a film-cutter in a Hollywood studio, a professional. Born after her mother's second—and last—marriage ended, Monroe was never certain who her father was.

"Tu Fu Watches the Spring Festival Across Serpentine Lake": In conception and many phrases, this version of Tu Fu's "Li-ren" is indebted to David Hawkes' *A Little Primer of Tu Fu* (1967).

"Little O": I mean for my title to echo Shakespeare's phrase for the Globe Theater in *Henry V*, "This wooden O." The argument here is with Stevens' "The Creations of Sound," his argument with Eliot.

"Collector": Lee Wiley's career, insofar as it flourished at all, thrived in the thirties, forties and fifties. This era—from screwball comedies to film noir, from Ella Fitzgerald and Duke Ellington to the Great American Songbook—remains the period that, for solace and pleasure, I most often return to. But it was also a suffocating box: what a relief to discover Antonioni and Satyajit Ray, Lowell and Ginsberg. They were part of a moment that, to my mind, was not Post-Modernist but Neo-Modernist, a movement that was not a repudiation of Modernism's seriousness and ambition, but a reinvention—a continuing attempt to discover what Modernism left out.

F.B.